Read-About® Math

How Much Does It Hold?

By Brian Sargent

Consultants
Chalice Bennett
Elementary Specialist
Martin Luther King Jr. Laboratory School
Evanston, Illinois

Ari Ginsburg
Math Curriculum Specialist

Children's Press®
A Division of Scholastic Inc.
New York   Toronto   London   Auckland   Sydney
Mexico City   New Delhi   Hong Kong
Danbury, Connecticut

Designer: Herman Adler Design
Photo Researcher: Caroline Anderson
The photo on the cover shows milk being poured into a glass.

Library of Congress Cataloging-in-Publication Data

Sargent, Brian, 1969-
    How much does it hold? / by Brian Sargent.
        p. cm. — (Rookie read-about math)
    ISBN 0-516-24957-6 (lib. bdg.)   0-516-29812-7 (pbk.)
    1. Volume (Cubic content)—Juvenile literature. 2. Mensuration
—Juvenile literature.   I. Title. II. Series.
    QA465.S27 2006
    530.8—dc22
                                                                2005019649

CHILDREN'S PRESS, and ROOKIE READ-ABOUT®,
and associated logos are trademarks and/or registered trademarks
of Scholastic Library Publishing. SCHOLASTIC and associated logos
are trademarks and/or registered trademarks of Scholastic Inc.

1 2 3 4 5 6 7 8 9 10 R 15 14 13 12 11 10 09 08 07 06

Water is everywhere.
We drink it. We take
baths in it. We swim in it.

Do you have drinking glasses in your house?

Do you have a fish tank or a bathtub?

Did you ever wonder how much liquid (LIK-wid) these containers can hold?

Let's start at the beginning.

This is one drop of water. It is very small.

This teaspoon is also small. How many drops of water can it hold?

It takes about 100 drops of water to fill this teaspoon.

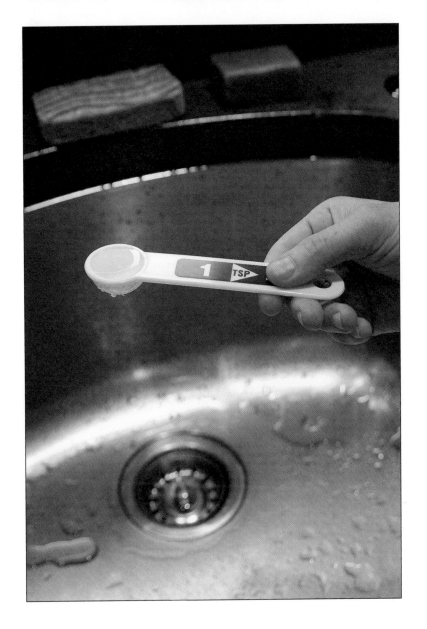

A tablespoon is bigger
than a teaspoon.

How much bigger is it?

Three teaspoons
fill one tablespoon.

This is a cup. How much
liquid can a cup hold?

Fill it with tablespoons
of water to see.

Sixteen tablespoons
fill one cup.

14

Many things at the grocery store are sold in pints.

This is a pint of cream.
It takes two cups to make one pint.

What is bigger than a pint? A quart is bigger than a pint.

People sometimes buy quarts of juice. A quart holds two pints.

SPOUT

PUSH UP HERE

PUSH UP HERE

THANK YOU
FOR SELECTING
BOICE BROS. DAIRY
PRODUCTS

TO OPEN

100% ORANGE JUICE
FROM CONCENTRATE K

Nutrition Facts
Serving Size 8 fl. oz. (240mL)
Servings Per Container 4

Amount Per Serving

Calories 110

% Daily Value*

Total Fat 0g	0%
Sodium 25mg	1%
Potassium 480mg	14%
Total Carbohydrate 27g	9%
Sugars 23g	
Protein 0g	

Vitamin C 130%

Not a significant source of calories from
fat, saturated fat, cholesterol, dietary
fiber, vitamin A, calcium and iron.
*Percent Daily Values are based on a 2,000
calorie diet.

**CONTAINS: WATER AND ORANGE
JUICE CONCENTRATE.
CONTAINS ORANGE JUICE
CONCENTRATE FROM FLORIDA
AND BRAZIL**

DISTRIBUTED BY
BOICE BROS. DAIRY, INC.
36 O'NEIL ST., KINGSTON, N.Y. 12401
PLANT NO. 36-2985

**KEEP REFRIGERATED
SHAKE WELL BEFORE SERVING
USE BY DATE SHOWN FOR BEST
FLAVOR.**

32 FL. OZ. (QUART) 946mL

7 49822 00700 1

18

Milk often comes in a gallon jug.

How much can a gallon hold? It holds four quarts.

If you play sports, you may use a water cooler.

This cooler holds 10 gallons.

I hope you are thirsty!

21

What holds more than
a cooler?

A bathtub can hold more
than a cooler. Many
bathtubs hold about
50 gallons.

That would be the same
as five 10-gallon coolers.

Let's go swimming!

How much water can
a swimming pool hold?

The water of 5,000
bathtubs would fill this
huge swimming pool.

25

Try measuring liquids yourself.

How many cups of liquid can your kitchen sink hold?

How about your soup bowl?

How about your tummy?

Words You Know

cup

gallon

measuring

pint

quart

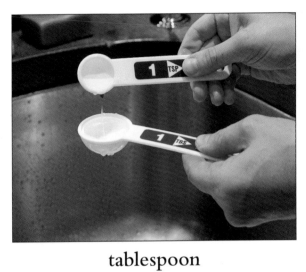

tablespoon

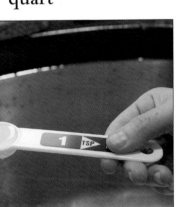

teaspoon

water

Index

About the Author

Brian Sargent is a middle-school math teacher. He lives in Glen Ridge, New Jersey, with his wife Sharon and daughters Kathryn, Lila, and Victoria. His kitchen sink holds about 7 gallons of water.

Photo Credits

Photographs © 2006: Corbis Images: 6 (John M. Roberts), 5 top (Norbert Schaefer); Getty Images: 21 (Chris Mueller/Stone), 22 (Barry Rosenthal/The Image Bank); ImageState: 3, 31 bottom right; Louise Lamson: 9, 10, 13, 26, 29, 30 top left, 30 bottom left, 31 top right, 31 bottom left; PhotoEdit: 14, 30 bottom right (Bill Aron), 5 bottom (Tony Freeman); Superstock, Inc.: 18, 30 top right (Francisco Cruz), 25 (Stefan Mokrzecki), cover (Sucre Sale); The Image Works/Dion Ogust: 17, 31 top left.